CHICKEN LITTLE
Count-to-ten

By MARGARET FRISKEY

Pictures by KATHERINE EVANS

 CHILDRENS PRESS, CHICAGO

Chicken Little went out to see the world.

He walked and walked until he was tired.

He wanted a drink.
He did not know how to get a drink.

He met one cow.
"How do you drink?" asked Chicken Little.
"I walk into the river up to my knees and
drink," said the cow.

one
1

Chicken Little walked into the river up to his knees.
"This is no place for me!" said Chicken Little.

Chicken Little met two elephants.
They were picking up water with their trunks.

two
2

Chicken Little tried to pick up water with his nose.
He could not breathe.

Chicken Little met three camels.
"How do you drink?" asked Chicken Little.
"We drink a lot but not often," said the camels.

three
3

The camels walked away.

Chicken Little met four colts.
"How do you drink?" asked Chicken Little.
"We draw the water through our lips,"
said the colts.

four
4

Chicken Little tried to draw the water through his lips. He could not drink.

Chicken Little met five pigs.
They had their heads in a trough
up to their ears.

five
5

Chicken Little put his head in a trough
up to his ears. He could not drink.

Chicken Little met six toads.
"How do you drink?" asked Chicken Little.
"We soak up water through our skins,"
said the toads.

six
6

Chicken Little tried to soak up water through his skin. "There must be a better way," said Chicken Little.

Chicken Little met seven monkeys.
They picked up little cups and drank.

seven
7

Chicken Little could not pick up a cup.

Chicken Little met eight kittens.
"How do you drink?" asked Chicken Little.
The kittens did not say. They were playing with
a ball of string.

eight

8

Chicken Little got caught in the string.

Chicken Little met nine puppies.
They were fighting over an old shoe.

nine

9

Chicken Little walked on and on.
"I must remember how chickens drink," he said.

Chicken Little met ten foxes.
"How do you drink?" asked Chicken Little.
"Why should we drink when we can have
chicken for our dinner?" asked the foxes.

ten
10

Chicken Little ran all the way home.

There was a pan of water under the pump.
"I will try once more to get a drink," said
Chicken Little.

A drop of water hit him on the head.
Chicken Little tipped his head back
and said, "Hey!"

Another drop ran down his throat.
"Why, of course!" said Chicken Little. "I must
tip my head back and let the water run down hill.
That is the way that chickens drink."